CARVING WOODEN
SANTAS
ELVES & GNOMES

By Ross Oar

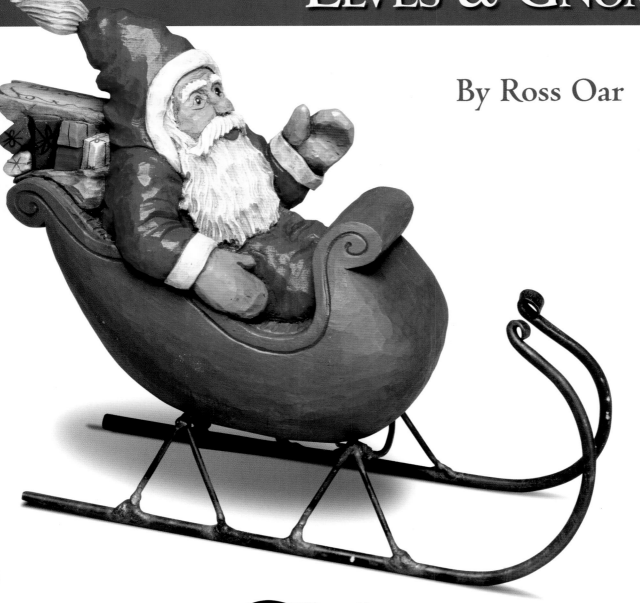

Fox
Chapel Publishing

1970 Broad Street • East Petersburg, PA 17520
www.FoxChapelPublishing.com

© 2008 by Fox Chapel Publishing Company, Inc.

Carving Wooden Santas, Elves & Gnomes is a compilation of projects featured in *Christmas Heirloom Patterns for Woodcarving: Volume I* and *Christmas Heirloom Patterns for Woodcarving: Volume II*, as well as new material. This edition was first published in 2008 by Fox Chapel Publishing Company, Inc. The patterns contained herein are copyrighted by the author. Readers may make copies of these patterns for personal use. The patterns themselves, however, are not to be duplicated for resale or distribution under any circumstances. Any such copying is a violation of copyright law.

Bibliographical note
Carving Wooden Santas, Elves & Gnomes is a revised and expanded republication of *Christmas Heirloom Patterns for Woodcarving: Volume I*, originally published in 1995, and *Christmas Heirloom Patterns for Woodcarving: Volume II* originally published in 1996. This edition of the work includes expanded instructions for getting started, new step-by-step instructional chapters with full-color photos, and 7 new projects.

Note from the author
I was glad to have some of my out-of-print Santa projects resurrected in this volume, and to have the chance to add carving and finishing tips to each one. I hope you enjoy the book!

Acknowledgments
Thanks to my editor, Kerri Landis, for helping to shape the book into what it is.

ISBN 978-1-56523-383-6

Publisher's Cataloging-in-Publication Data

Oar, Ross.

    Carving wooden Santas, elves & gnomes / by Ross Oar. -- 1st ed. --
    East Petersburg, PA : Fox Chapel Publishing, c2008.

       p. ; cm.

       ISBN: 978-1-56523-383-6
       Subtitle on cover: 28 patterns for hand-carved Christmas
    ornaments and figures.
       "Revised and expanded republication of 'Christmas heirloom
    patterns for woodcarving: volume I', originally published in 1995,
    and 'Christmas heirloom patterns for woodcarving: volume II'
    originally published in 1996."--T.p. verso.

       1. Wood-carving--Technique. 2. Wood-carved figurines--
    Patterns. 3. Christmas decorations--Patterns. 4. Santa Claus--Art.
    5. Elves--Art. 6. Gnomes--Art. I. Title. II. Christmas heirloom
    patterns for woodcarving.

TT200 .O27 2008
745.594/12--dc22   2008

To learn more about the other great books fromFox Chapel Publishing, or to find a retailer near you,
call toll-free 800-457-9112 or visit us at *www.FoxChapelPublishing.com*.

Note to Authors: We are always looking for talented authors to write new books in our area of woodworking, design, and related crafts. Please send a brief letter describing your idea to Acquisition Editor, Fox Chapel Publishing, 1970 Broad Street, East Petersburg, PA 17520.

Printed in China
10 9 8 7 6 5 4 3 2 1

CONTENTS

Getting Started

Tools and Materials

I use a variety of carving tools to make the projects in this book, though you could get by with a few different sizes of #9 gouges, a carving knife, and a V-tool. Other miscellaneous materials you will need to make the projects in this book include: tracing paper, medium and fine sharpening stones, a leather strop, acrylic paint, and brushes. I used the paint palette pictured on page 5 to create the colors on my carvings. Be sure to keep tools sharp at all times: a sharp tool makes a sharp carving.

Supplies and some roughed-out basswood blanks are available. All rough-outs are made from Ross' originals. For information write: West Falls Woodcarving, 7458 Ellicott Road, West Falls, N.Y. 14170.

These are a few of the tools you will see me using throughout the book. From left to right: 2 mm #9 gouge, 6 mm #9 gouge, 10 mm #9 gouge, 8 mm 75° V-tool, 8 mm #9 gouge, 10 mm 90° V-tool, 12 mm #9 gouge, micro V-tool, all-purpose carving knife, and sharp-pointed detail knife.

Carving Hints

Start your carving by tracing the pattern on your basswood block or wood of preference, using both the side and the front views. Make sure the figure is positioned so the wood grain runs vertically. If you have a band saw, cut out your blank or use a power or hand saw that will enable you to make your cutout. After you have your cutout, start to round off the edges of the wood with your carving knife and large gouges. Draw on the wood in pencil before you carve a specific area. Take your time, keep your tools sharp, and check the photograph and pattern frequently to make sure you are taking off the correct areas of wood. Remember to strop your knife after every 15 minutes of carving; this will keep your knife edge sharp and prevent the frustration caused when trying to carve with a dull knife. I suggest that you go through the two step-by-steps first for guidance. Woodcarving is a very rewarding hobby that you will find very relaxing; with practice, you will advance through the difficulty levels of the projects in this book and continue to improve your carving skills. Have fun!

Note about band saw patterns: Though I do not use them myself, band saw patterns—the dotted lines around the front and side views of each pattern—were provided to help you create a carving blank. If you don't want to have much waste to carve away, try creating your band saw blank using the line of the actual pattern. However, the band saw pattern itself can be a valuable tool for the beginning carver.

Design Hints

After carving Santas from this book, you may be inspired to create your own special carvings from scratch. I'll tell you how I design my carvings in case you ever want to create your own.

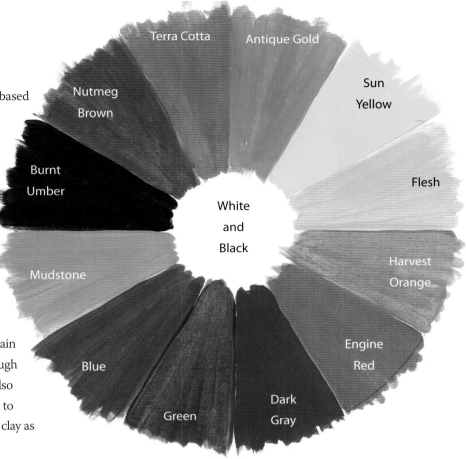

Many times when I create a Santa, it is based on my observations or experiences of something happening at a special time. One example is "Santa's Day Off," which was inspired while watching the luge event in the winter Olympics.

When designing a new Santa, I do several thumbnail sketches of different poses. When I've finalized the poses, I make the final drawing of the full profile and face views. This pattern is then transferred to the appropriate size block of wood with the grain running the proper direction, usually through the length of the piece. Quite often I will also model in clay, which allows more freedom to move and tweak the design. I then use the clay as a model to carve from.

Painting and Finishing Tips

When the carving is completed, I use acrylic paint washes to finish the project. I use washes because you can always go back and add a layer to darken the shade, but with undiluted paint, you are stuck with the end result. To make a wash, put a small amount of paint on your palette and start mixing water in until the color is diluted. I do not seal my carvings before I paint them. When painting, I usually cut in with a #000 and then fill the balance in with a #2 or #5 brush.

To paint skin tones, I use a flesh wash. Before the paint dries, I use a dry brush to stipple small amounts of a red and orange mixture on high spots like the cheeks, nose, ears, chin, and forehead.

For eyes, use a very fine #000 brush to paint white on the entire eyeball. With a deep blue or burnt umber, put in the iris after the white is dry.

When the pupil is totally dry, create a highlight: take a pin, fine awl, or toothpick, touch the tip in undiluted white paint, and touch the left or right side of eyeball (be sure to pick the same location in both eyes).

On the red areas, while the paint is still wet, create shadows in low spots (wrinkles, under arms, etc.) by stippling with a darker red.

When the carving is completely dry, apply three coats of MinWax clear satin or similar finish. Be sure to get in all the cracks, and to wait until each coat is dry before putting on the next one. When the polyurethane is completely dry—24 hours or more—apply a light wash of burnt umber artist oil paint (in a tube), linseed oil, and paint thinner over the carving. Immediately wipe the entire carving with an old T-shirt or cloth. If the color collects in cracks, you can dry brush those areas before the finish dries. This finish creates an antique effect that tones down the paint and gives a nice overall finish.

Christmas Gnome

MATERIALS AND TOOLS

- 2¾" x 2½" x 5" basswood block
- Band saw
- Carving knife
- 6mm #9 gouge
- 10mm #9 gouge
- 10mm 90° V-tool
- 12mm 90° V-tool (Optional)
- 8mm 75° V-tool
- #3 ⅝" gouge
- 5mm #9 gouge
- 2mm #9 gouge
- #5 ¼" gouge

This carving was originally created for a beginner carving class. You can create variations by changing the type of hat the gnome is wearing. It can also be made into a small Santa if you carve a ball on the top of the hat, or carve a traditional Santa hat.

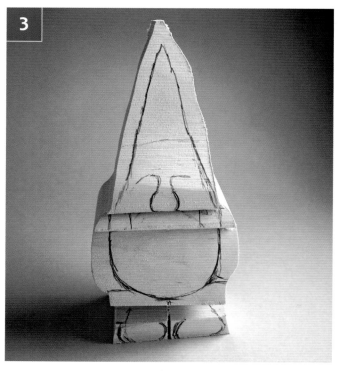

Use tracing or carbon paper to transfer the front and side band saw patterns (the dotted line around the carving patterns on page 7) onto a wood block. Be sure that the grain runs vertically.

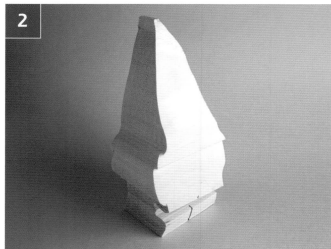

Use a band saw to create the blank. Cut the side with least curves first, but don't complete the cut. Leave about ⅛" of material uncut along the first cut to keep the waste attached; this provides a flat surface, which eases the cutting of the second profile. When both sides are cut, separate the waste from the blank.

From Santa's Bag

If the pattern has acute angles that are difficult to cut on the band saw, I go around them and carve them later. I like to make the blank slightly bigger than the pattern, which allows room for adjustments while carving.

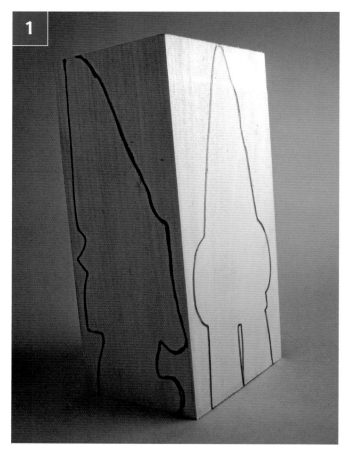

Using the carving patterns on page 7 as reference, pencil rough outlines onto the blank.

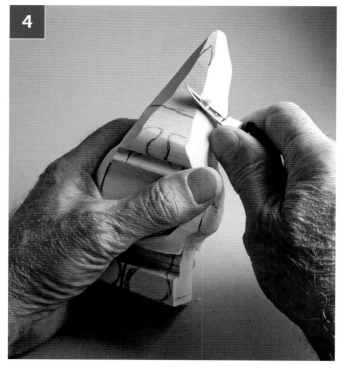

Working around the figure, round off sharp corners with a knife.

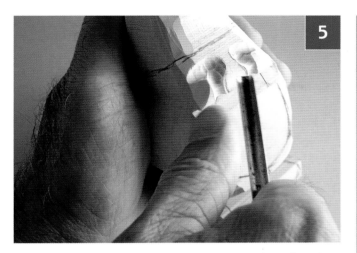

Carve the eye sockets with a 6mm #9 gouge. Cut along the sides of the nose and rough in the location of the face.

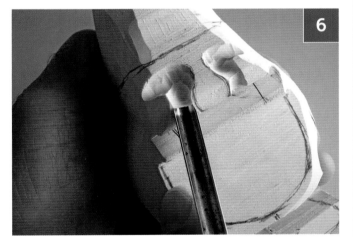

Using the 6mm #9 gouge, cut deeper along the nose and define the cheeks.

Use your knife to round all the corners. Next, begin texturing with a 10mm #9 gouge; cut across the grain.

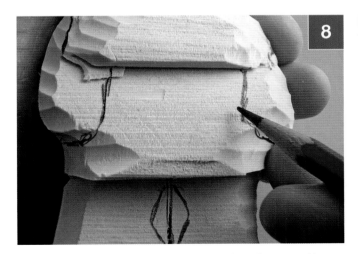

Pencil in all the hard lines for the hat, arms, beard, ears, and legs.

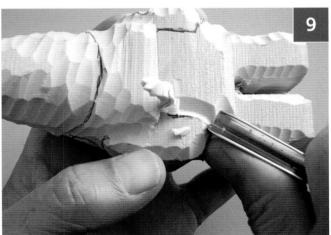

Use a 10mm 90° V-tool to cut in all of the hard lines. Use the 10mm #9 gouge to cut across all newly exposed grain.

This is how the back of your carving should appear after cutting the hard lines with the V-tool.

Pencil in the tops of the boots and cut them with the V-tool.

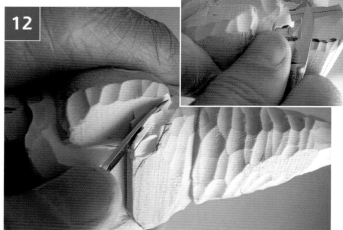

Knife cut the back of the hair and the corners of the legs.

Pencil in the mustache and mouth; use the 10mm or a 12mm V-tool to outline the rough details on the face. Use the 10mm #9 gouge to rough out the face and beard.

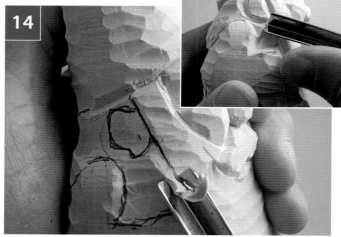

Pencil in the ears and arms. Outline the beard, sideburns, and ears with an 8mm 75° V-tool.

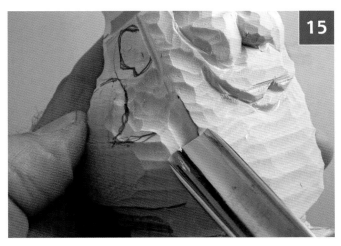

Free the hands from under the beard with the 10mm #9 gouge. Use the 10mm 90° V-tool to cut out the inside edges of the arms.

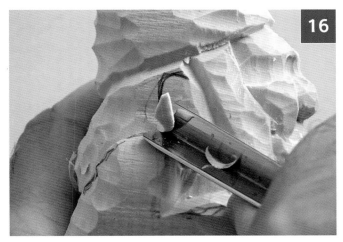

Cut the shoulders with the 10mm 90° V-tool.

Round out the legs with the 10mm #9 gouge. Cut out the coat edge using the carving knife.

Use the knife to separate the thumbs from the rest of the hands. Notice the cuts made to rough out the figure.

Use the knife to start putting in more detail. Outline the ear; create shadows wherever possible. This brings the carving to life.

20

Put wrinkles in the hat with the knife; this can also be done with a V-tool. Carve off the flat surface of the hair.

21

Further shape the arms, body, and boots. Re-cut the tops of the boots and define the cheek and hairlines.

From Santa's Bag

When I carve, I like to move around the figure making small cuts to shape the complete carving. It gives me a better idea of what the figure should look like.

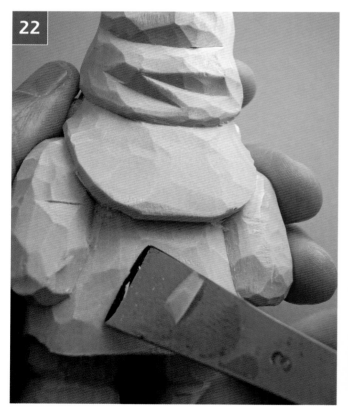

22

Smooth the coat, arms, hair, and beard using a #3 ⅝" gouge. Smooth the entire carving, working toward final detail cuts. Shaping can also be done with a knife.

23

Shape the foot of the boot with the 10mm #9 gouge around the toes. Note the shadow cut I made with the knife on the top of the boot.

Point the boot and shape the foot size with the knife. Add wrinkles in the boots and pants.

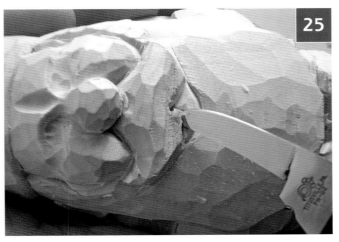

Form the mustache. Also use a triangle cut to create an opening in the mouth to create a shadow.

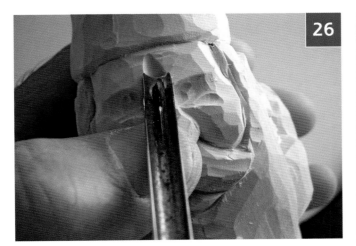

Use a 5mm #9 gouge to cut a groove from the top of the nose to the bottom of the cap. This makes a starting point for creating the eyebrows.

Using the knife, cut the eyebrows as shown.

Here is what the gnome should look like at this point.

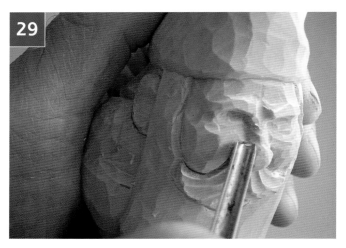

29

Clean the eye sockets and shape the nose with the 5mm #9 gouge.

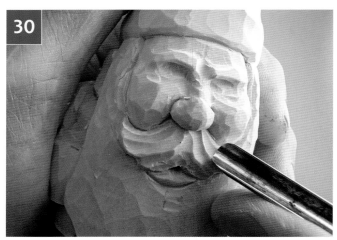

30

Use the 5mm #9 gouge to put in the first pass of cuts forming the hair on the mustache. Follow with a 2mm #9 gouge to make finer cuts.

31

Create a shadow cut along the side of the nose using a #5 ¼" gouge.

32

Carve detail on the beard. Use the 10mm #9 to make the first cuts; then, cut over that with a mid-size gouge (5mm or 6mm #9); finish up with the 2mm #9. Be sure that your cuts are random and do not form any particular pattern. Carve the gnome's hair in the same manner as the beard.

From Santa's Bag

When the gouge chips curl up at the bottom of the hat, I cut them off with a knife. Don't try to pull them off!

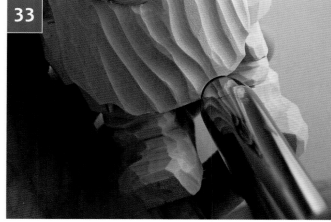

33

Using different size #9 gouges (10mm, 5mm, 2mm), cut straight in at the bottom of the hairline in the back to create the natural look of hair.

Add detail to the mustache with the #9 gouges.

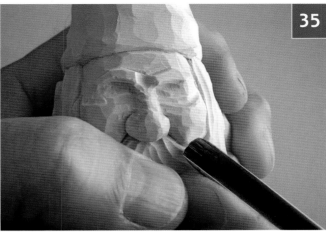

Use the 8mm 75° V-tool to make shadow cuts on the cheeks next to the mustache.

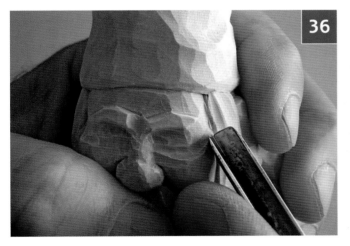

Shadow cut along the hairline around the face with the 8mm 75° V-tool.

Pencil in the eyes. I always do the left one first so I can line up the other eye better. Try drawing the eyes on a piece of paper and see what works for you.

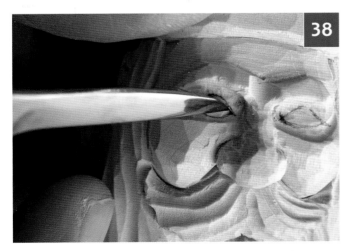

Using a very sharp pointed knife, make a triangle cut in the corners of the eyes and carefully remove the triangle.

Draw the knife along the top and bottom pencil eye lines, cutting a sliver out to create the eyeball.

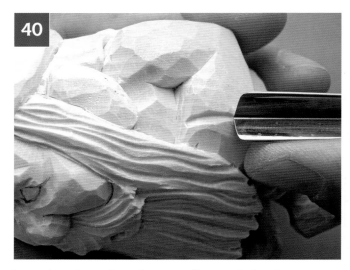

40

Using the 90° V-tool, cut the coat cuff. Leave the hand partway under the beard.

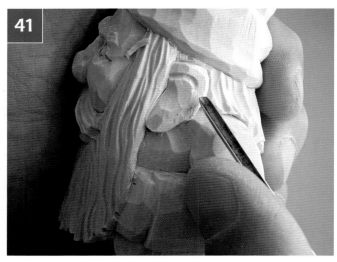

41

Using the 2mm #9 gouge, cut out a groove to create the earlobe.

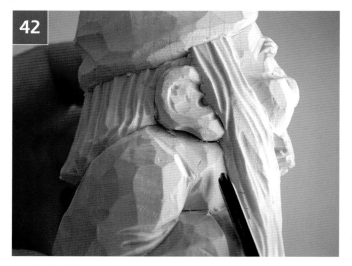

42

Use the knife to carve away the inside of the ear. The ear has also been outlined with the knife to create more shadows.

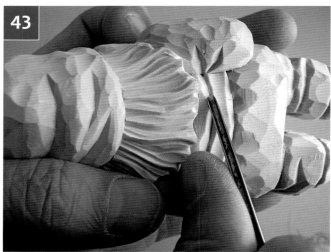

43

To create the back belt, use the 90° V-tool and the knife. Use an 8mm #9 gouge to make the tucks under the belt.

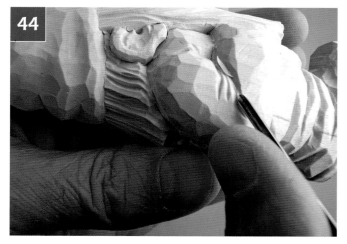

44

Use a 90° V-tool to create wrinkles in the coat at fold points, such as elbows. Then, make the wrinkles deeper with a knife.

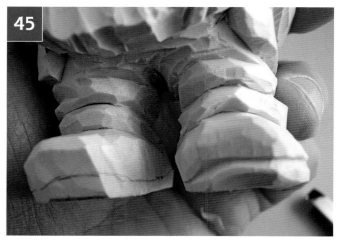

45

Pencil in the soles of the boots and use the 10mm 90° V-tool to delineate the soles.

46

Undercut the sole at the toe to give the foot a more natural-looking curve.

Your completed gnome should look like this. Now you are ready to paint.

From Santa's Bag

To create the wash for the gnome's coat and hat, begin with a dab of yellow ochre on the palette. Add water, then a touch of brown, and then a touch of green. Play around until the shade is pleasing to you.

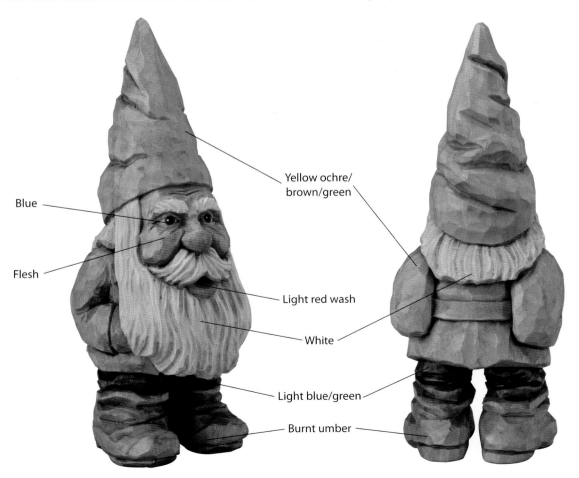

Blue

Flesh

Yellow ochre/
brown/green

Light red wash

White

Light blue/green

Burnt umber

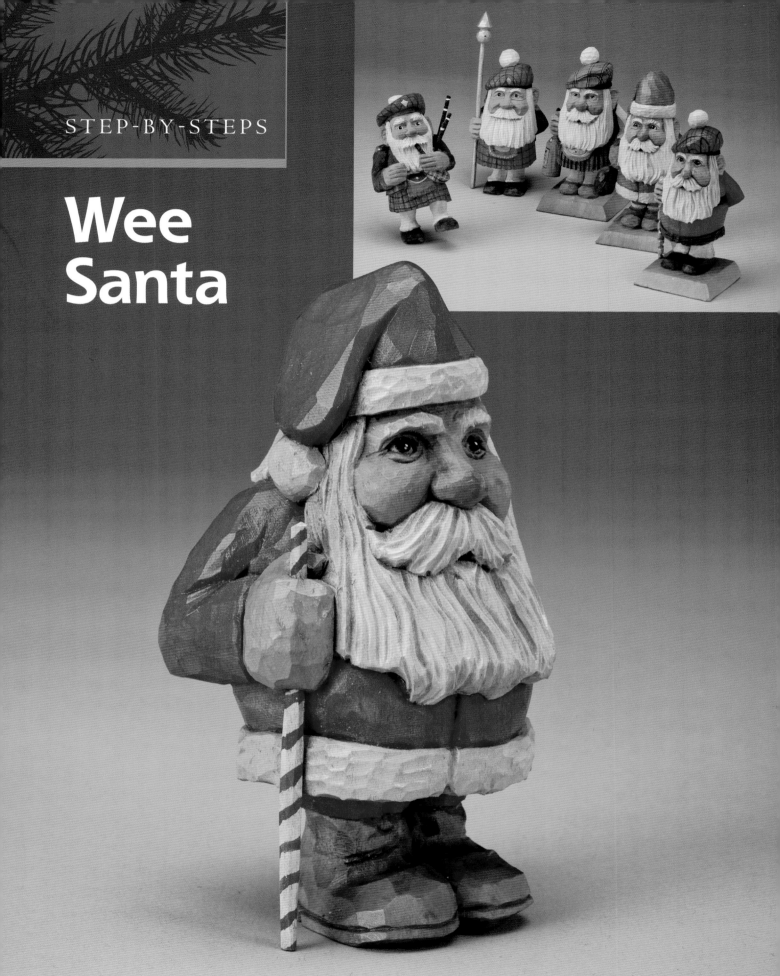

STEP-BY-STEPS

Wee
Santa

MATERIALS AND TOOLS

- 3" x 3" x 6" long basswood block
- Band saw
- 10mm #9 gouge
- 8mm 75° V-tool
- 6mm #9 gouge
- 10mm 90° V-tool
- Carving knife
- 3mm #9 gouge
- 8mm #9 gouge
- 5mm #9 gouge
- 2mm #9 gouge

I designed the Wee Santa one Christmas when I needed to make nice gifts. This project makes a good gift because it's a good beginner project and also simple to create variations from. My mother was a Scot, which inspired some of the variations seen on page 18.

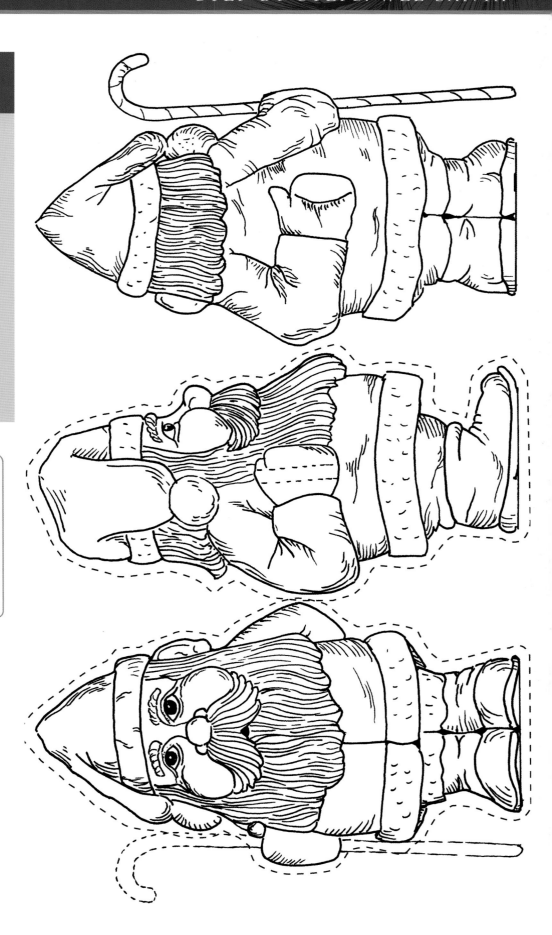

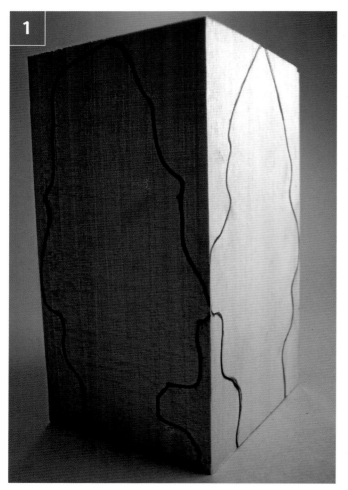

1

Use tracing or carbon paper to transfer the front and side band saw patterns (the dotted line around the carving patterns on page 19) onto a basswood block. Be sure that the grain runs vertically.

2

Use a band saw to create the blank. Cut the side with the fewest curves first, but don't complete the cut. Leave about ⅛" of material uncut along the first cut to keep the waste attached; this provides a flat surface, which eases the cutting of the second profile. When both sides are cut, separate the waste from the blank.

From Santa's Bag

If the pattern has acute angles that are difficult to cut on the band saw, I go around them and carve them later. I like to make the blank slightly bigger than the pattern, which allows room for adjustments while carving.

3

Start taking off the corners all around with a 10mm #9 gouge. This step begins the roughing out stage. Note: I drew some guidelines, using the pattern on page 19, to show where to make cuts.

Continue to use the 10mm #9 gouge to shape the basic figure. Keep shaping and rounding off to create the basic form, referring to the patterns and photographs provided.

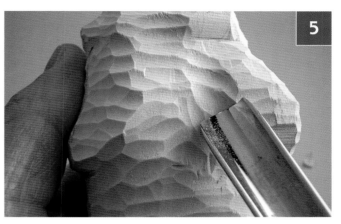

Left side showing more shaping still using the 10mm #9 gouge.

Rough out the left arm, which is behind the back.

Rough out the right arm.

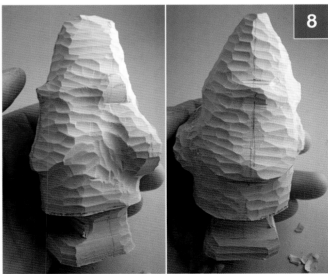

Your rough-out should look something like this at this point. This view shows the left side of the arm, ear, nose, and beard. The insets show the front of the figure and the top of the hat. All cuts should be worked to the center line so the face is not flat.

9

Draw in the hard lines of the face, hat, tassel ball, and arms using the carving patterns on page 19 as reference.

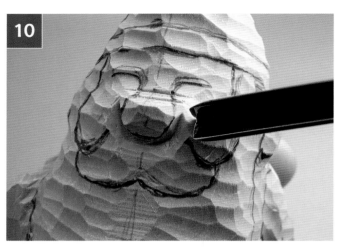

10

Cut around the nose using an 8mm 75° V-tool.

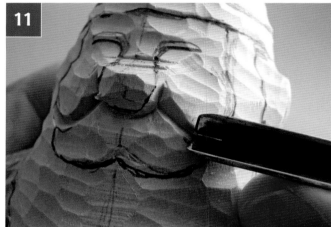

11

Use the 75° V-tool to cut the top of the mustache into the sides of the nose.

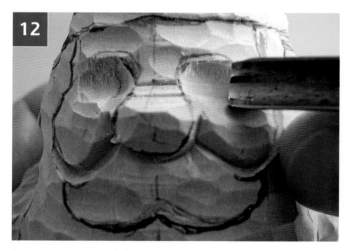

12

Finish cutting around the cheeks with the V-tool. Use a 6mm #9 gouge to rough in the eye sockets.

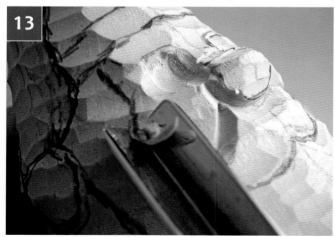

13

Define the sides of the face and sideburns with a 10mm 90° V-tool.

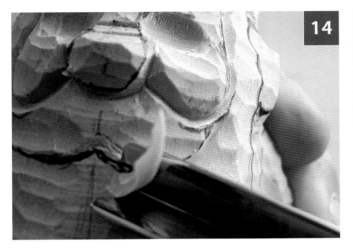

Undercut the mustache with the 8mm 75° V-tool.

The undercut of the mustache is completed. Note how the face should look at this point in the process.

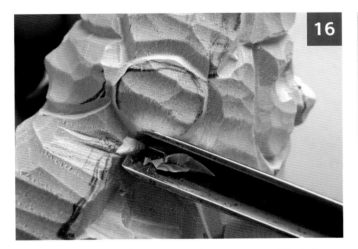

Use the 8mm 75° V-tool to create outline cuts around the hat brim and ball.

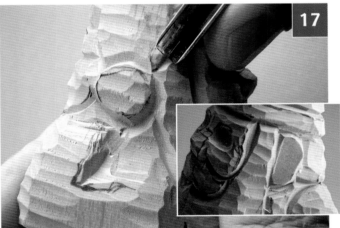

Cut the outside of the beard and the ear with the 8mm 75° V-tool.

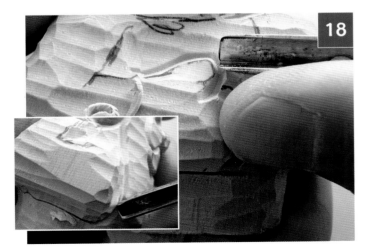

Continue using the 8mm 75° V-tool to rough out the hands and arms.

Cut the side of the temple straight in using the 10mm #9 gouge.

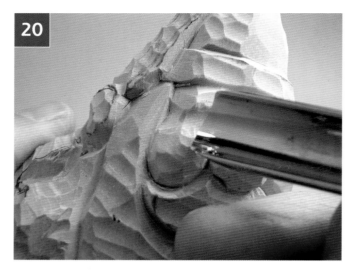

Shape the face into the sideburn using the 10mm #9 gouge. This step makes the cheek stand out.

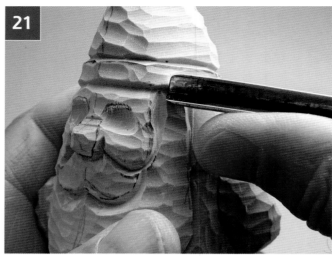

Deepen the cuts of the hat cuff with the 8mm 75° V-tool.

Using a knife, round the cheeks.

Start using the knife to round out and clean up the carving.

Undercut the nose to create shadows.

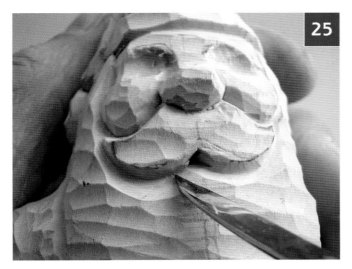

With the knife, create a triangle cut at the mouth to give more shadow.

Continue carving off rough edges around the figure with the knife.

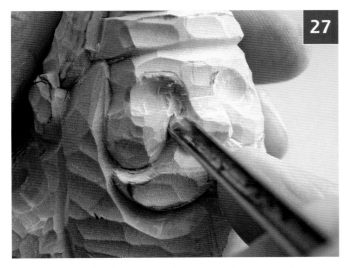

Cut along the side of the nose with a 3mm #9 gouge up into the edge of the eye.

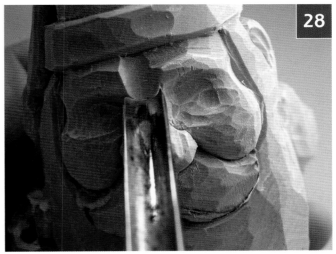

I used the 6mm #9 gouge to cut just above the nose up to the hat brim. This creates the space between the eyebrows.

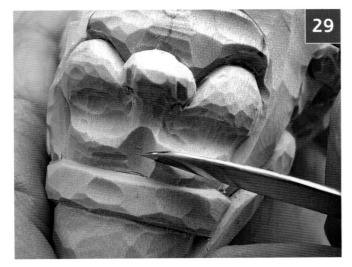

Make knife cuts at the top of the brow to create the forehead.

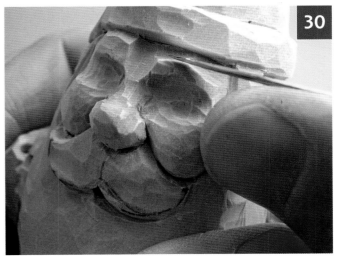

Use the knife to define the eyebrows.

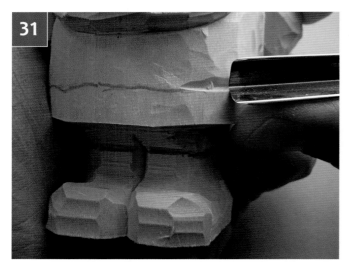

Use the 10mm 90° V-tool to cut in the fur trim on the coat.

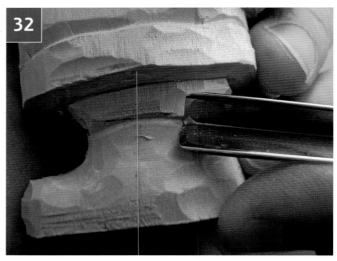

Continue using the 10mm 90° V-tool to cut in the tops of the boots.

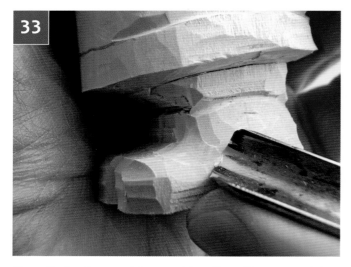

Shape the boots around the toe with an 8mm #9 gouge, and then switch to the knife to finish shaping.

Using multiple small cuts, cut across the grain with a 5mm #9 gouge to create the look of fur trim.

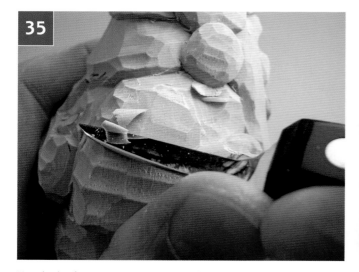

Use the knife to create a smooth surface all over the figure.

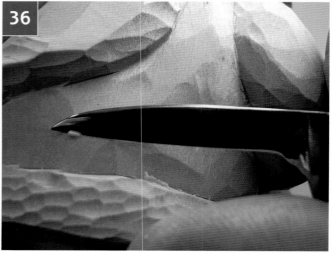

Make a stop cut up to the fur trim with the knife.

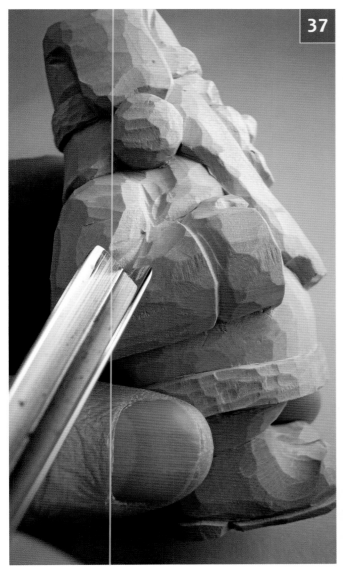

Use the 10mm 90° V-tool to create more detail in the wrinkles and folds. Also, cut cuffs onto the coat.

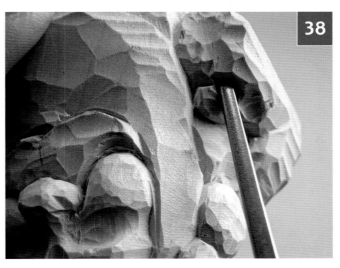

Use a 2mm #9 gouge to cut a hole through the right hand for the walking stick.

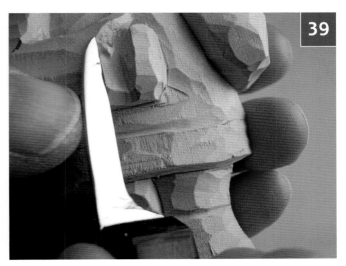

Shape the back hand with the knife.

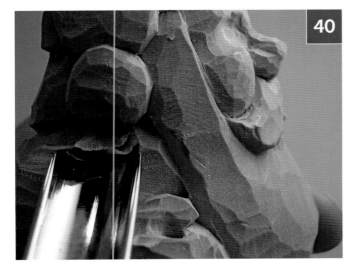

Use the 10mm #9 gouge to cut in deeper shadows on the shoulder under the hat ball.

From Santa's Bag

Deeper cuts, like the ones performed in Step 40, create shadows that make the carving look more realistic and three dimensional.

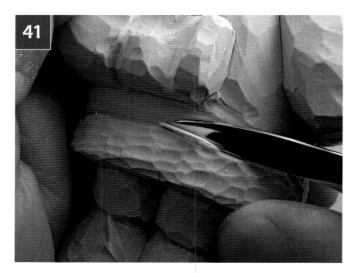

Make your finishing cuts with the knife.

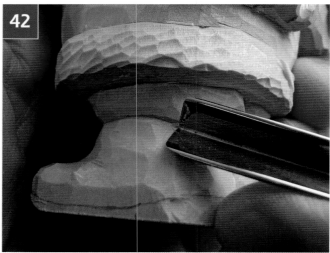

Use the 10mm 90° V-tool to put finishing cuts at the top of the boots.

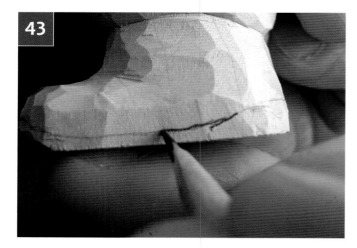

Pencil in the soles of the boots.

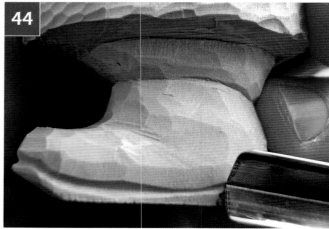

Using the 10mm 90° V-tool, cut in the soles and heels of the boots.

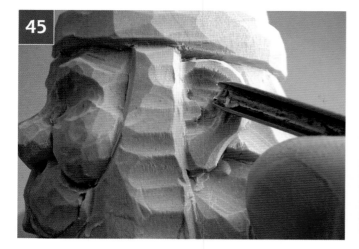

Carve the inside of the ear with the 3mm #9 gouge.

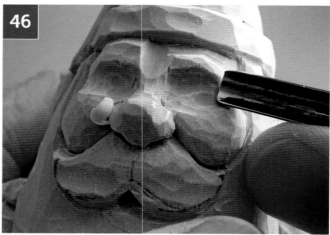

Open up the eye socket area with the 5mm #9 gouge.

Pencil in the eyes with a fine point pencil.

Create triangle cuts in the corners of the eyes with the knife. Poke the knife into each corner and make two cuts at an angle: one down and one up. This will make the eye a football shape. Lastly, make a slight sliver cut to make the eyeball really stand out.

From Santa's Bag

Drawing the eyes works best for right-handers if the left eye (as it appears to the artist) is drawn first. Try sketching the eyes on a piece of paper and see what works for you.

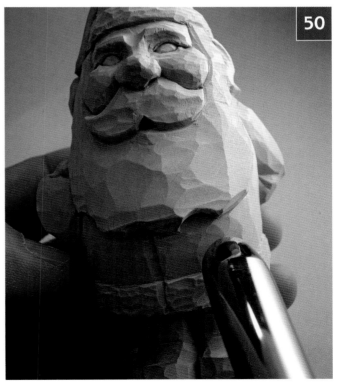

Create fur trim on the hat using the technique from Step 34 on page 26.

Flip the 10mm #9 gouge so the convex surface is on top. Cut along the bottom of the beard and the hair straight in at 90° to create a natural curved shape.

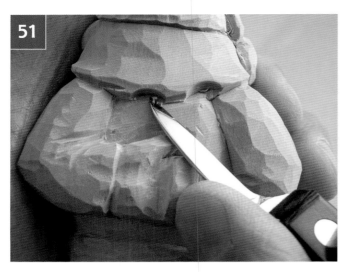

51

Remove any curls from the gouge cuts with the knife.

52

When cutting the hairlines, use three #9 gouges: I use the 10mm, 6mm, and 2mm. First, make random cuts with the 10mm; then, follow up using the 6mm; finish with the 2mm.

From Santa's Bag

Be sure not to make straight cuts while texturing the hair; curve the strands randomly so they look realistic. Also, creating shallow and deep cuts makes for good shadows, which will also add to the realism.

53

On the mustache, I used two sizes of #9 gouges: 6mm and 2mm. First, make the 6mm cuts, and then follow up with the 2mm gouge. Also, use a micro V-tool to create the finished cuts over and under the eyes.

This is what my finished, unpainted Wee Santa looks like with the walking stick in place. To create the walking stick, take a piece of basswood and cut down the length of it ³⁄₁₆" from the corner. Make another cut to create a ³⁄₁₆" x ³⁄₁₆" length of stick. Round off the ends with the knife, and shape it to your satisfaction.

To create the variations on the Wee Santa, as seen on page 18, follow the instructions below.

A **Spearhead:** Use a knife to carve the tip of the spear separately; glue onto shaft. Use a ³⁄₁₆" drill bit to make a hole through the hand.

B **Sporran:** Use a micro V-tool to create the fringes on the sporran (pouch worn on front of kilt).

C **Bagpipes:** The pipes are carved separately and glued in. Carve light lines onto the bagpipe to help with painting the fine lines.

D **Hat:** The Scottish hat is carved with a knife. The ball is undercut with a 75° V-tool and textured to look like fur (see Step 34). After painting, draw on lines with a fine or medium felt tip black marker.

E **Bottle:** The bottle of Scotch was carved separately and glued into the hand. The back half is flat so it fits against the body. The top of the bottle is carved with the hand.

Kilt: Use an 8 or 10mm 75° V-tool to make the pleats. Undercut them like you did with the beard using the 75° V-tool. After painting, draw on lines with a fine or medium felt tip black marker.

F **Spiral walking stick:** Pencil the spiral on and then cut the marks off with a 3mm #9 gouge. Create a tenon to fit the stick into the hand. The top of the stick is carved with the hand. Use a 75° V-tool to cut in the top of the stick.

Spats: Using a 5mm #9 gouge, cut straight in to create flaps on the spats (the covering over the shoes). A #8 or #9 micro gouge, such as a Ramelson or Flextool, will create the buttons.

G **Bag:** Carve the bag separately with a knife and glue it into the hand. The top of the bag is carved with the hand.

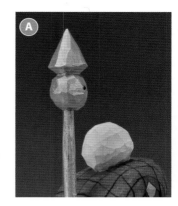

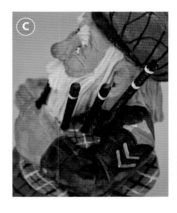

Bright red

Brown

Flesh

White

Gray

Burnt umber

White

Red

Santa
Star
Ornament

Star can be painted red and white, or gold leaf. Glue the head onto the star. Use a small eye screw to attach a hook. I make hooks out of wire or paper clips by bending them with needle-nose pliers.

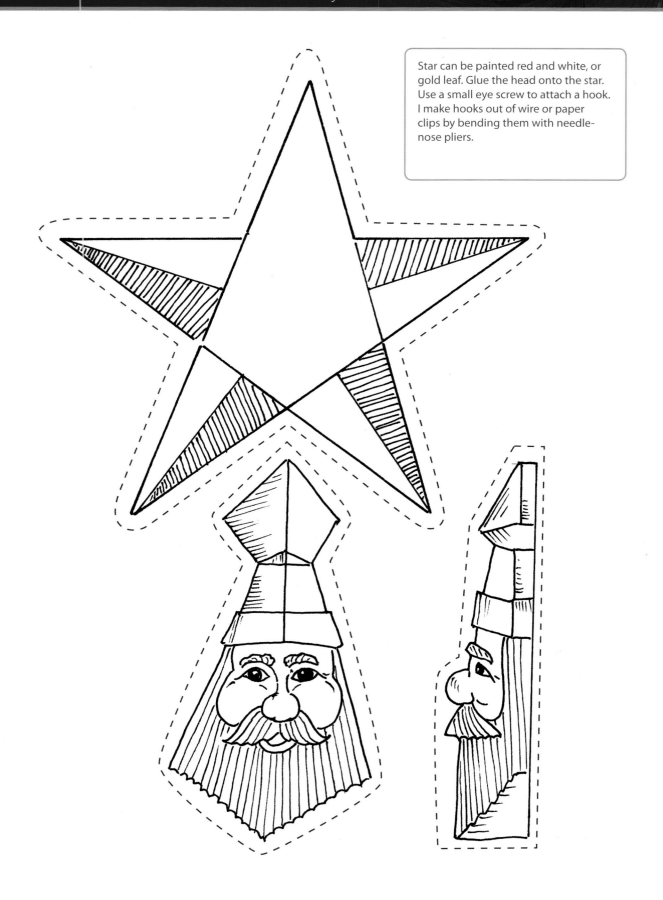

Miniature Father Christmas

Carve a hole in the pack to glue gifts or keep closed as shown. Customize this project by altering the paint colors.

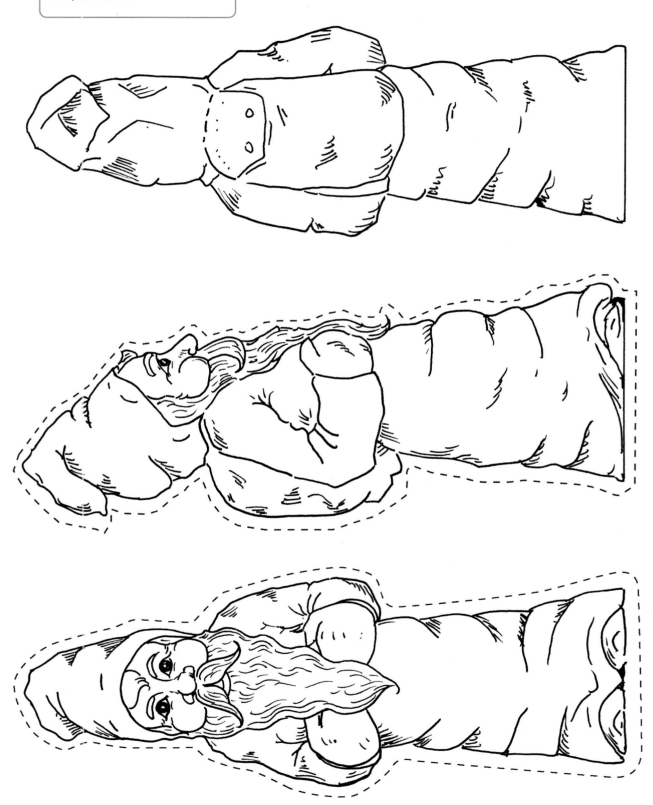

Customized Santa

To customize your Santa's hat, use the pattern ideas at right. To make a roly poly from this pattern, remove the legs at the dotted line.

Russian

Old Fashioned

Viking

Ski Hat

Monk

Dotted line for roly poly option

Rocking Chair Santa

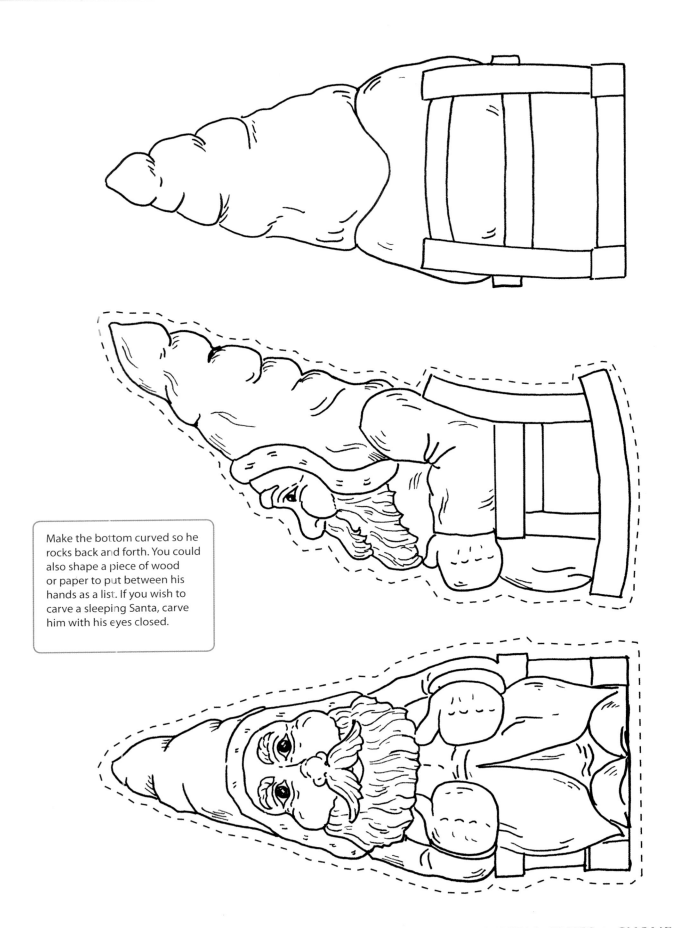

Make the bottom curved so he rocks back and forth. You could also shape a piece of wood or paper to put between his hands as a list. If you wish to carve a sleeping Santa, carve him with his eyes closed.

Waving Santa

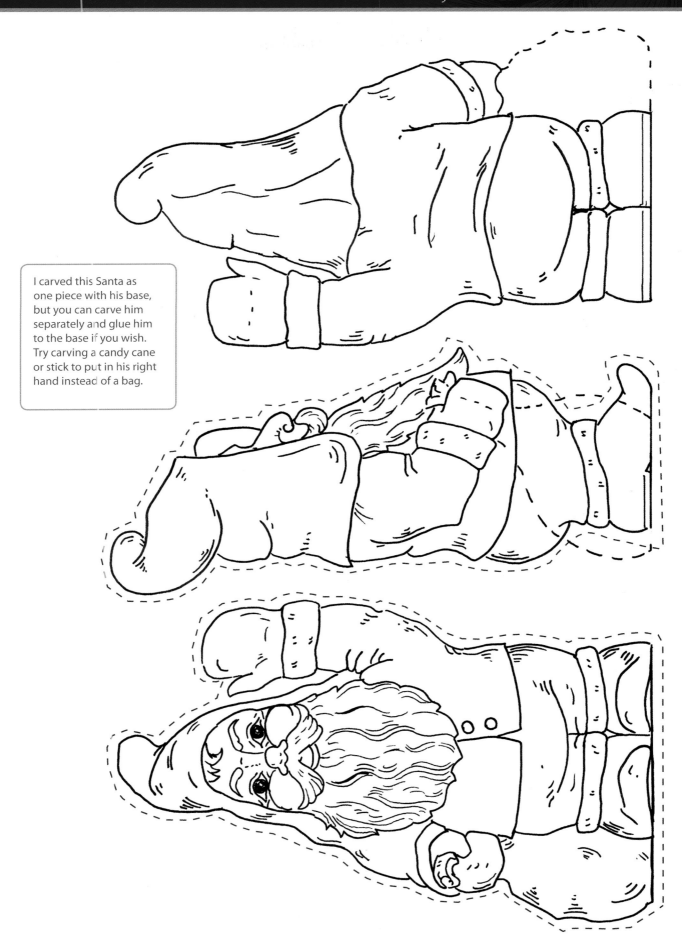

I carved this Santa as one piece with his base, but you can carve him separately and glue him to the base if you wish. Try carving a candy cane or stick to put in his right hand instead of a bag.

Old World Santa

This Santa is fairly easy to do and is good for gifts. To add rocking motion, curve the bottom of the piece.

Roly Poly Santa Head

I originally designed this Santa for my grandkids. They loved making him bob and rock! I suggest screwing washers in the bottom to add weight.

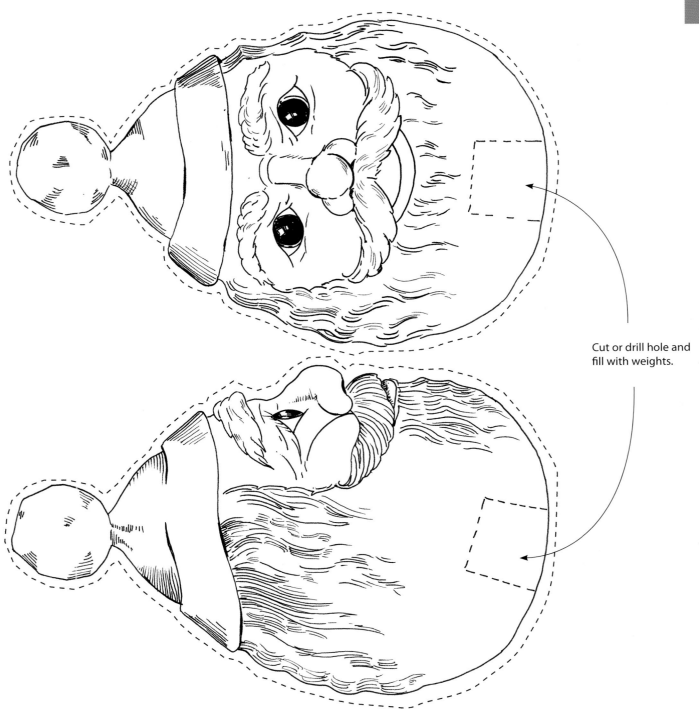

Cut or drill hole and fill with weights.

Pattern appears at 75% of actual size

Santa Awaits the Big Day

To create a mountain man Santa, carve a buckskin fringe and high boots, and add a powder horn. To make a dozing Santa, carve his eyes closed as shown below.

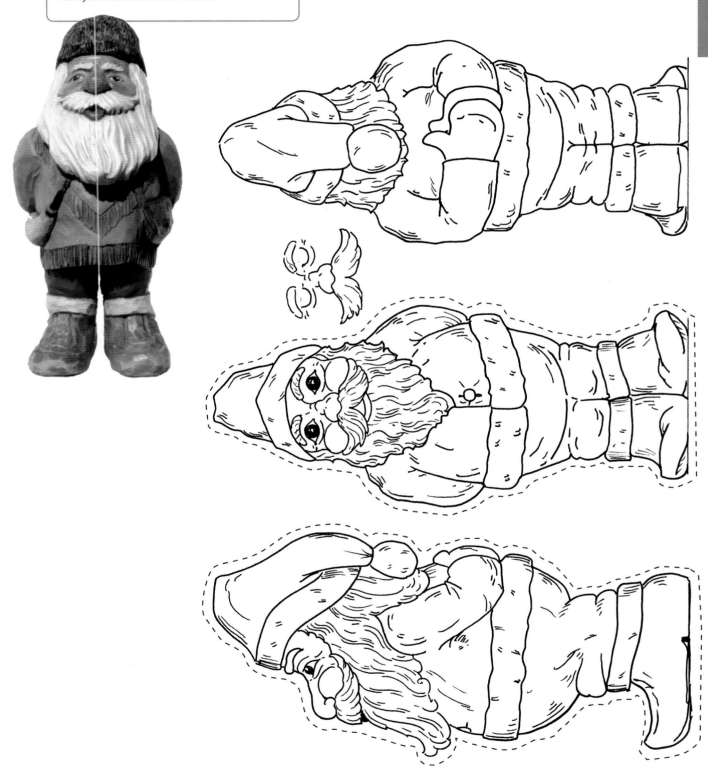

Pattern appears at 75% of actual size

Toy
Soldier

Add your own touches when painting: spats, medals, etc. Carve gun separately and add after painting. Drill hole in hand for gun.

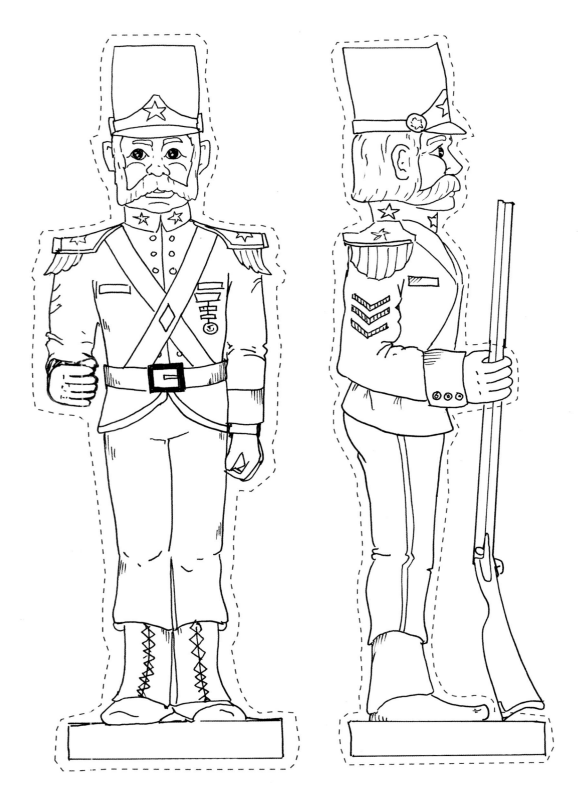

Pattern appears at 75% of actual size

Santa Makes His List

The list and the figure are carved together. Customize the list with your family's and friends' names by writing with a felt pen before varnishing.

MERRY CHRISTMAS

JEN
ERIC
ROSS

Pattern appears at 75% of actual size

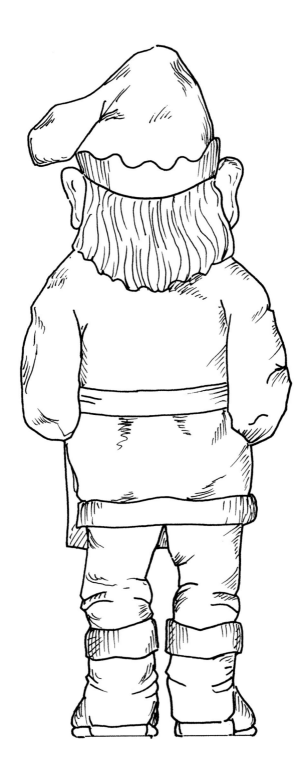

Pattern appears at 75% of actual size

Father Christmas

I created this design with a bell in its hand, but you could replace it with a bag or other object of your choosing. I carved this Santa as one piece with his base, but you can carve him separately and glue him to the base if you wish. Be aware that carving it as one piece requires a lot of work with the knife.

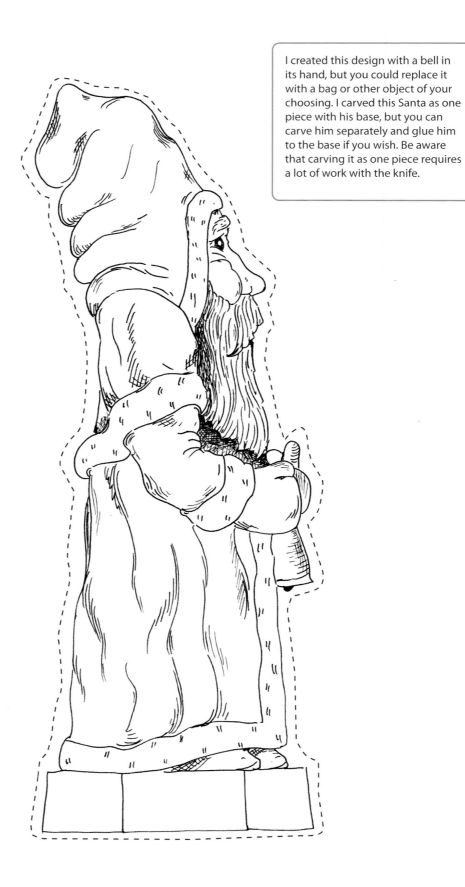

Pattern appears at 75% of actual size

Pattern appears at 75% of actual size

Spiral Santa Ornament

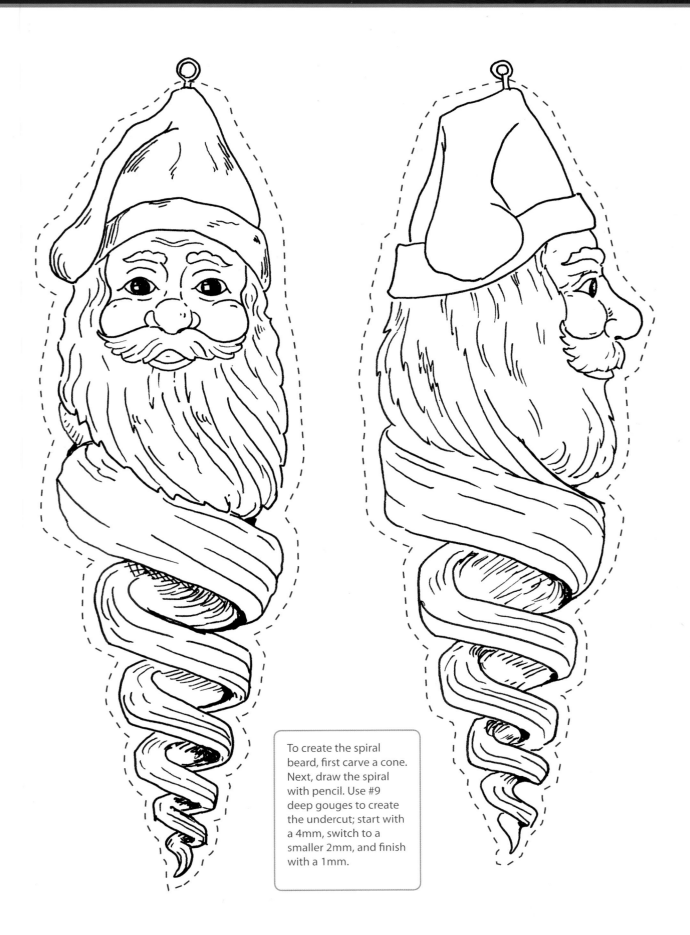

To create the spiral beard, first carve a cone. Next, draw the spiral with pencil. Use #9 deep gouges to create the undercut; start with a 4mm, switch to a smaller 2mm, and finish with a 1mm.

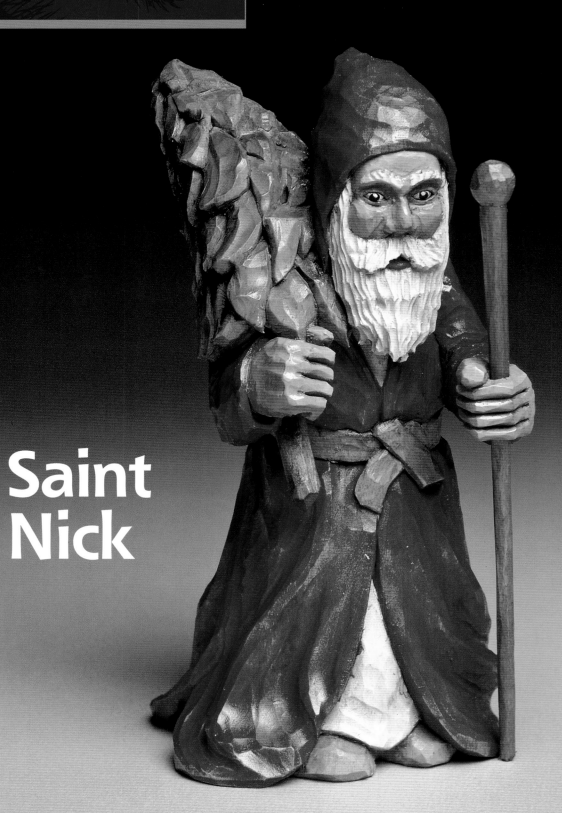

Saint Nick

Tree trunk and walking stick
are carved separately and
added after painting. You
could also carve a bag in his
hand instead of a stick.

INTERMEDIATE

Santa's Elf

The stool is made separately. A candy cane, hammer, or other object can be put in his hand. The elf can also ride Santa's Reindeer, page 90.

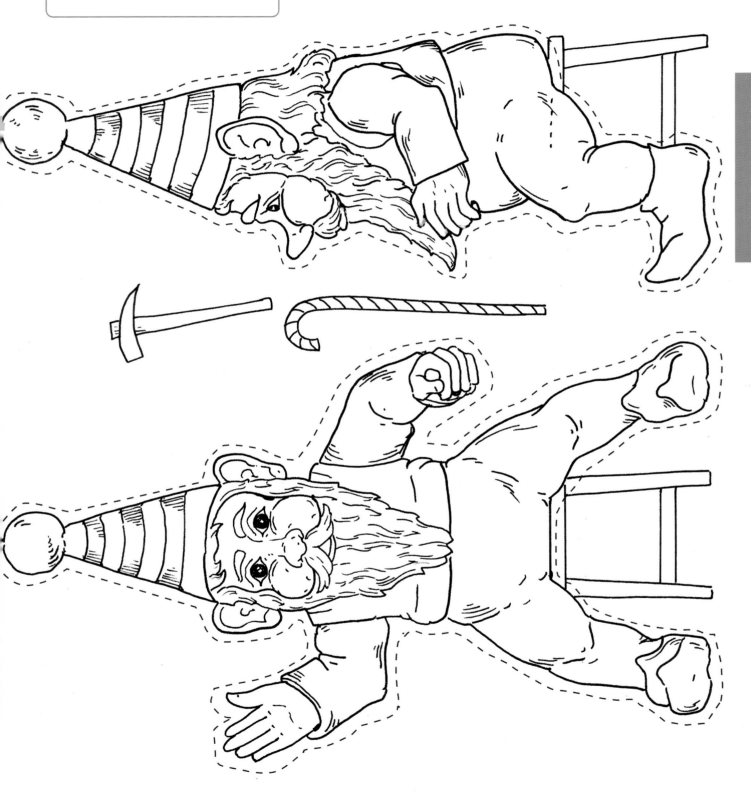

Mrs.
Claus

To make the head positionable, push a sharp X-Acto knife into the neck along the dashed lines; the head can be put into different positions by slightly twisting the neck. I've carved the basket with apples for feeding the reindeer, but you could carve Santa's lunch.

Pattern appears at 75% of actual size

Elf
Ornament

I was in a comical mood when I designed this elf.
The balls on our Christmas tree seemed to need
something—like an elf hanging on for dear life! You can
change the pattern on the ball. Try stripes, polka dots,
or Santa hats. Use a small eye screw to attach a hook. I
make hooks out of wire or paper clips by bending them
with needle-nose pliers.

INTERMEDIATE

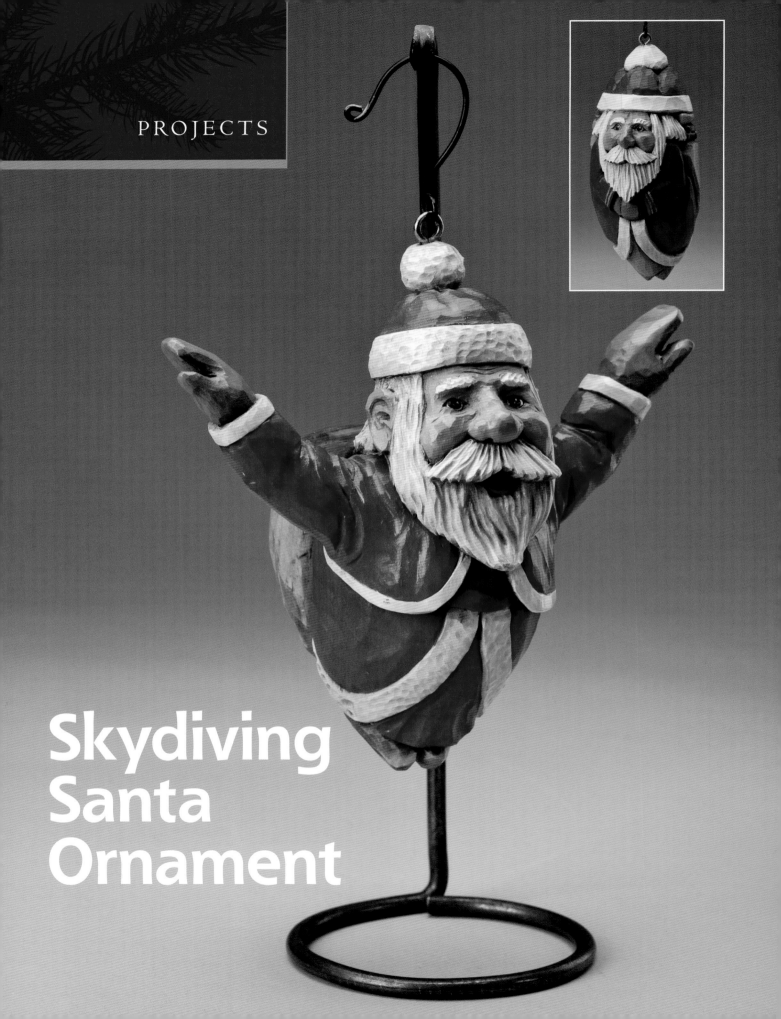

Skydiving Santa Ornament

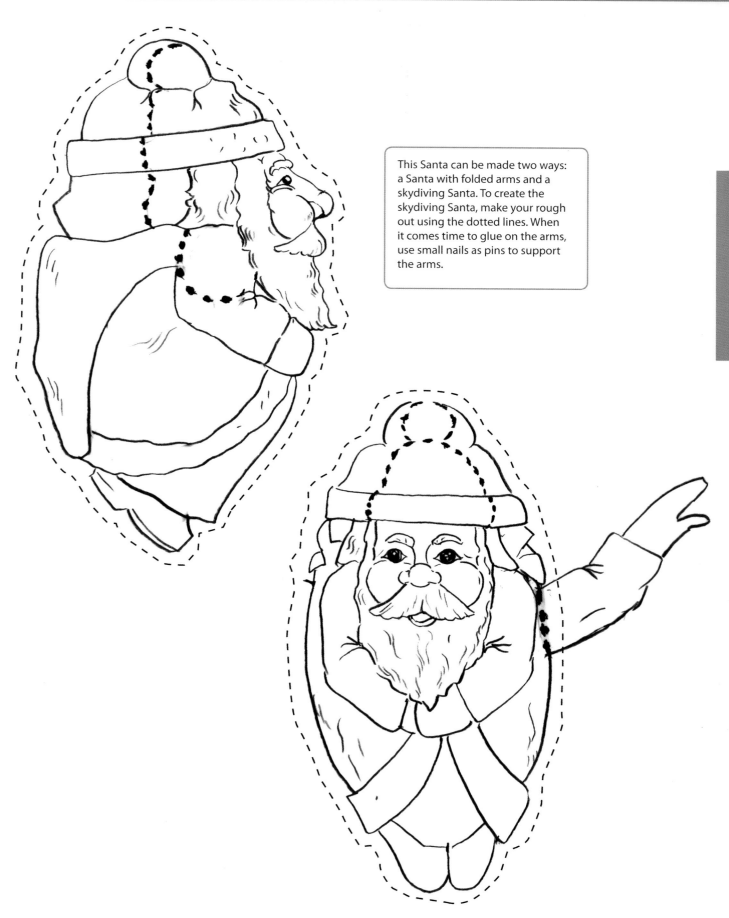

This Santa can be made two ways: a Santa with folded arms and a skydiving Santa. To create the skydiving Santa, make your rough out using the dotted lines. When it comes time to glue on the arms, use small nails as pins to support the arms.

Santa Claus with Toys

You can add more toys to the bag on this Santa's back. Just make sure you leave the blank big enough to fit them all! Try carving a steam engine or a doll with its arm hanging out of the bag.

Pattern appears at 75% of actual size

INTERMEDIATE

Carve a doll or other
item and insert it here.

To add eyeglasses, bend
a paper clip as shown here.

Pattern appears at 75% of actual size

Candle Santa

INTERMEDIATE

I designed this Santa to remind the viewer of a church service with candles. His book could be a Bible or another book. The gown was influenced by the base of a Tiffany-style stained-glass lamp. Be very careful when carving the delicate flame.

Pattern appears at 75% of actual size

Pattern appears at 75% of actual size

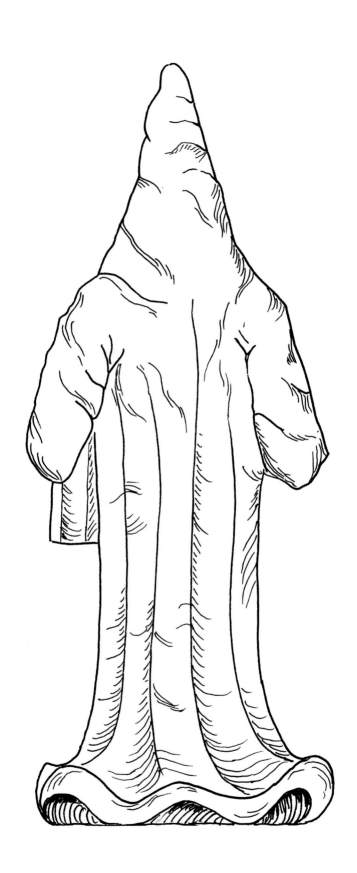

Pattern appears at 75% of actual size

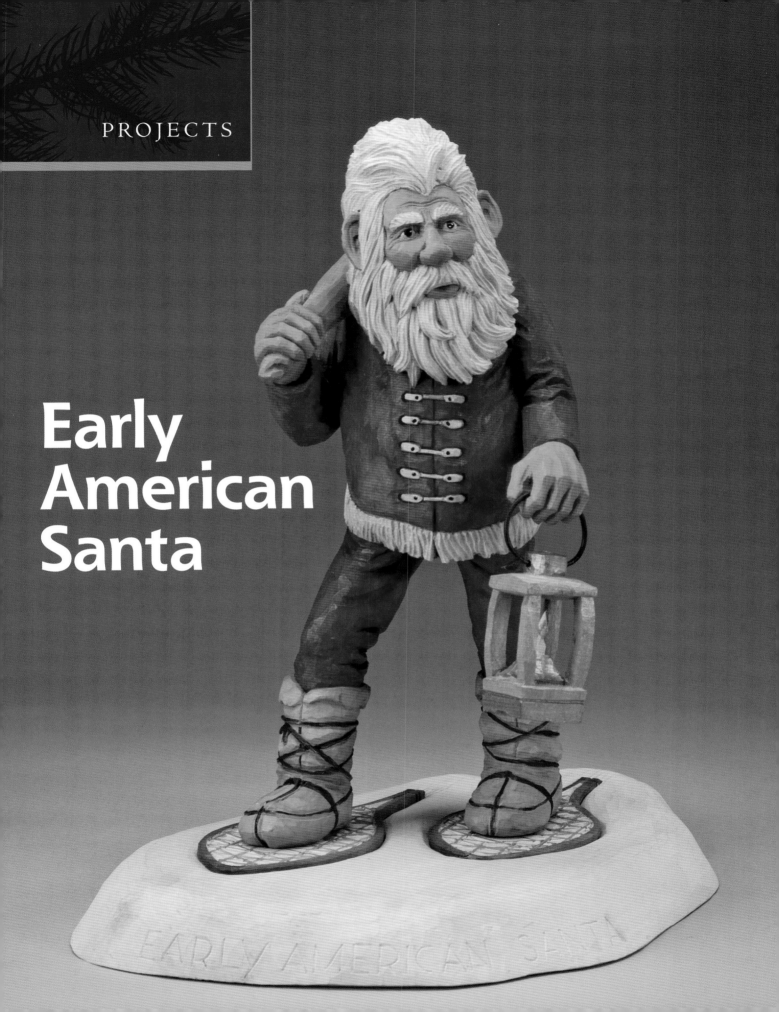

Early American Santa

The lantern is carved separately and added to the hand with wire. The snowshoes are also carved separately and glued on. Use a gouge to cut around the shoes on the base so they will look like they are sinking into the snow.

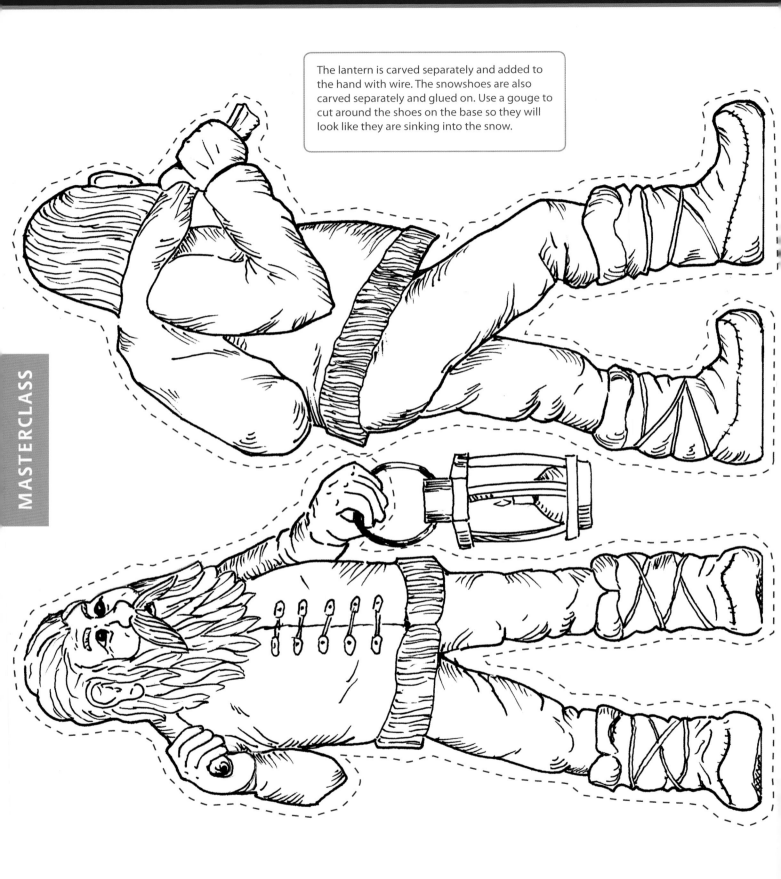

Pattern appears at 75% of actual size

Pattern appears at
75% of actual size

CARVING WOODEN SANTAS, ELVES & GNOMES

Santa
on Sled

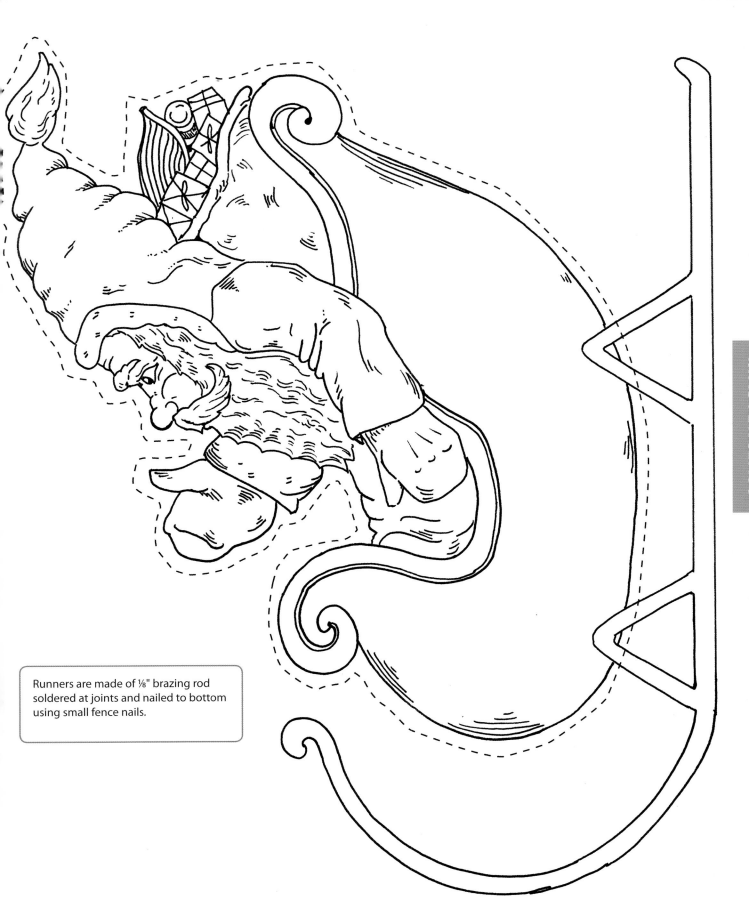

Runners are made of ⅛" brazing rod soldered at joints and nailed to bottom using small fence nails.

MASTERCLASS

Fence Nail

Checking it Twice

To make eyeglasses, bend a paper clip as shown on page 70. Santa's list is made of curved and painted tin-can material. Be sure to file or bend all the edges to get rid of sharpness. Make legs and rocker by soldering welding rod together and gluing into bottom of seat. Can also be carved from wood.

MASTERCLASS

Feeding the Birds

I was inspired to create this Santa when I saw people feeding birds in a big city. Of course, it helped matters that my daughter saw me sketching it and wanted one.

This Santa can be a shelf sitter, or can sit on any box, bench, etc., that you can make or find.

Bird carved separately.

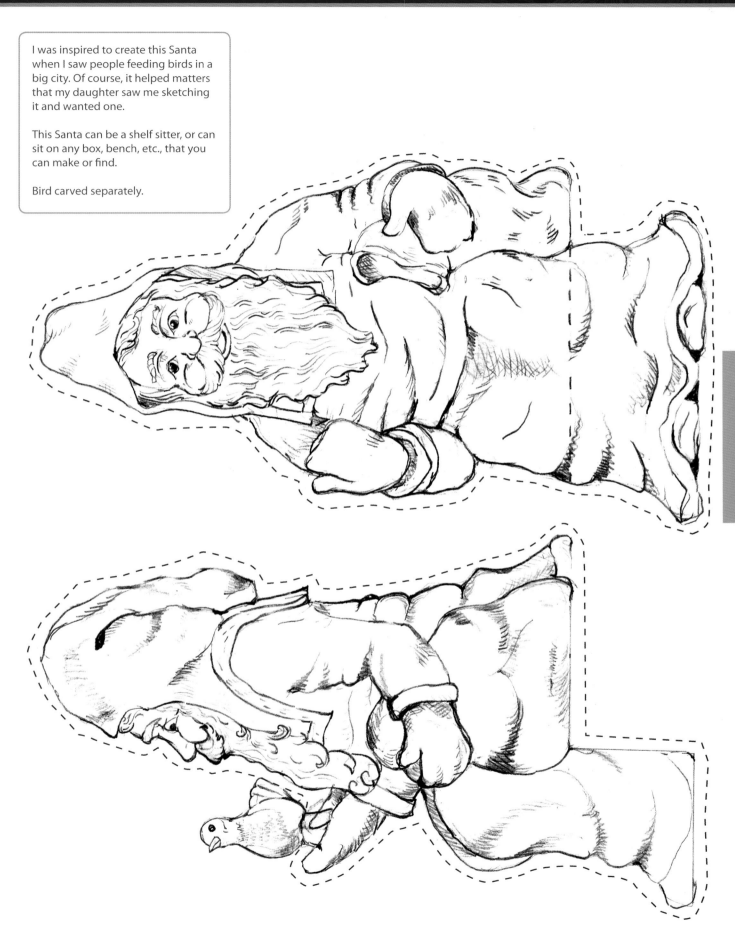

MASTERCLASS

Tree Cutter Santa

This is Santa out of his dress clothes! Use a small gouge to outline the footprints and a flat chisel or #3 gouge to clean them out. The tree trunk is attached to his hand.

Position the axe so it lies on his shoulder.

Tree and axe carved separately.

Pattern appears at 75% of actual size

Carve the tree so the tip touches the base when the stem is in his hand. Use a knife to cut small V-shaped marks to undercut the boughs. This creates lots of shadow and the appearance of real tree boughs. Then, use a 90º V-tool to create branch trim.

Pattern appears at 75% of actual size

Santa's Reindeer

When creating the antlers, make the big curve and then solder the small pieces onto the big curve. File the ends. The antlers are glued into half-inch deep holes in the head. To make the antlers look like real antlers, dip them in beige paint, let dry, and then brush spots with burnt umber. The brass bell can be bought from a hobby store. The elf from page 60 can sit on a reindeer.

Pattern appears at 75% of actual size

Pattern appears at 75% of actual size

Santa's Day Off

MASTERCLASS

Santa and luge top are one piece of wood and will require more wood removal than usual after band sawing.

Runners are made of coat hangers or carved separately from wood.

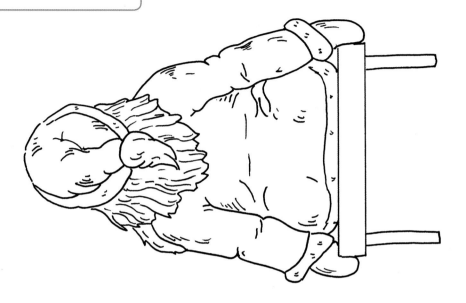

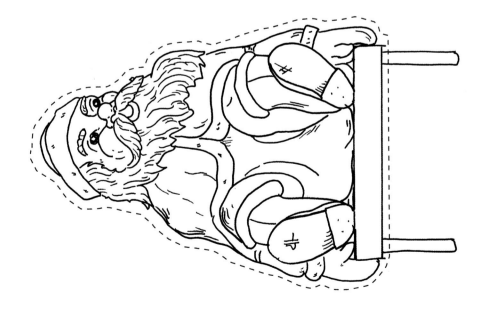

Pattern appears at 75% of actual size

Pattern appears at 75% of actual size

Rough-outs available for some patterns.

For ordering information, visit www.oarcarver.us or write to:
West Falls Woodcarving
7458 Ellicott Road
West Falls, NY 14170

The Oar Carver pocket knife is made of D2 steel, which holds its edge very well.

Wood carver pewter belt buckle designed by Ross Oar.

Discover More Great Woodcarving Books from Fox Chapel Publishing

Fine Art of Carving Lovespoons
Understanding, Designing, and Creating Romantic Treasures
By David Western

Learn to carve romantic gifts with 15 original patterns and 3 step-by-step projects. Includes a chapter on the history of this captivating craft and an inspiring gallery of spoons in a variety of styles.

ISBN 978-1-56523-374-4
$24.95 · 200 Pages

Relief Carving Wood Spirits
A Step-by-Step Guide for Releasing Faces in Wood
By Lora S. Irish

Learn the enjoyable craft of relief carving as you create 10 of your very own wood spirits. Carefully illustrated and thoroughly explained – from preparing the wood and transferring the pattern to evaluating the various carving cuts.

ISBN 978-1-56523-333-1
$19.95 · 136 Pages

Decorative Woodcarving
Accessories for the Home
By Fred Wilbur

Learn to carve traditionally designed projects for the home featuring beautiful architectural details, including an heirloom-quality jewelry box, bookends, and more with complete step-by-step projects.

ISBN 978-1-56523-384-3
$24.95 · 192 Pages

Halloween Woodcarving
Frightfully Fun Projects
By Cyndi Joslyn

Definitely a treat for any woodcarver! Offering 10 original patterns to carve whimsical Halloween-inspired characters including a mummy, witch, ghost and more. Includes basic woodcarving techniques and finishing secrets.

ISBN 978-1-56523-289-1
$16.95 · 128 Pages

Santa Showcase
Celebrate the Season with 24 Patterns from the Best of Woodcarving Illustrated
By Editors of *Woodcarving Illustrated*

The best Santa projects from the past 10 years of *Woodcarving Illustrated*, these 20 patterns and four step-by-step projects represent the craftsmanship of carving's top artists. Includes the cover Santa from the premiere issue of *Woodcarving Illustrated*.

ISBN 978-1-56523-340-9
$16.95 · 96 Pages

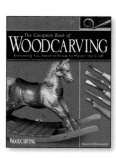

Complete Book of Woodcarving
Everything You Need to Know to Master the Craft
By Everett Ellenwood

Whether you're a woodworker expanding your talents, a seasoned carver refining your skills, or a beginner newly introduced to this enjoyable craft, this is the only carving book you need. Includes every classic style, including power carving, and contains 9 projects and helpful resource section.

ISBN 978-1-56523-292-1
$27.95 · 288 Pages

Look For These Books at Your Local Bookstore or Woodworking Retailer
To order direct, call **800-457-9112** or visit *www.FoxChapelPublishing.com*

By mail, please send check or money order + $4.00 per book for S&H to: Fox Chapel Publishing, 1970 Broad Street, East Petersburg, PA 17520